WALKLEY T

THE A

By Simon Dawson & Paul Scarrott

Books coming from DS Publishing in 2004

Walkley and Crookes Past and Present
Broomhill Past and Present
Worrall and Oughtibridge Past and Present
Hillsborough Past and Present

Printed and published by:

DS Print, Design & Publishing
286 South Road
Walkley
Sheffield S6 3TE
Tel: 0114 285 4050
Fax: 0114 285 3050
Email: info@dspad.co.uk
Web: www.dspad.co.uk

Based on the book 'A Short History of Walkley' by Albert Staley

ISBN 0-9546769-0-4

Published December 2003

Foreword

We set up *DS Print, Design & Publishing* in Walkley to offer a large variety of printing, graphic design, internet services and publishing. We became interested in the history of Walkley and it's people and tried to find a book on the subject. To our surprise we found nothing in print, so we decided to go ahead and produce this book, largely based on an original booklet produced for St. Mary's Church by Albert Staley.

Simon Dawson & Paul Scarrott

Acknowledgements

The old images contained in this book have been sourced from Sheffield Local Studies library. Special thanks to Mike Spick for organising this.

Photography: David A Dawson

Grateful thanks for help in the production of this book:

Sheila Dawson	Valentin Arhipov
Susan Dawson	Matthew Wall
Nada Ross	Anna Ellis

To all Sheffield authors...

DS Publishing is looking to publish books by local writers. If you have written or are going to write a book please contact us and we'll be happy to advise and may publish your book.

Contact us below:

DS Publishing
286 South Road
Walkley
Sheffield S6 3TE

Tel: (0114) 285 4050
Fax : (0114) 285 3050
Email: info@dspad.co.uk
Web: www.dspad.co.uk

Origins of Walkley

The name of the former village of Walkley comes from the old English 'Walcas Leah', meaning Walca's forest clearing. The people of Walkley, what few there were, were very hardy and kept good health, like the people of Crookes. This was because the village was built on the steep side of a hill, bleak and open to the continuous winds blowing across Rivelin and from the direction of Stanage Pole. The first few dwellings, mainly farm buildings and labourers' cottages, looked down the hillside to Rivelin Valley or to Neepsend where the River Don flowed.

The area was mainly scrubland and heavy woodland and most of these forests stretched over to Crosspool and Crookes. The open spaces like the Bolehills, Crookesmoor and Bell Hagg Common were used for grazing cattle and sheep. The Bolehills were also used for smelting iron; open furnaces were driven into the hillsides and outlets made to let out the smoke. These "boles" were replenished with wood from Rivelin and the surrounding woods which abounded with immense oaks, and thus became the "Bolehills".

It was reported that just after 1066 (The Conquest) the last Saxon Earl to fight William The Conqueror had a hall near Rivelin called Haugh Park. This was the famous Hall of Waltheof and he later made peace with William and married Judith, William's niece, in 1070. Later he started to build a wooden castle at the junction of the Don and the Sheaf at Lady's Bridge. After Waltheof's execution, through a conspiracy, a Norman named De Lovetot made improvements to the castle.

Early Roads

During this time there were only two roads in Walkley. The main one was the original Roman Road that came from Brough over Stanage Pole to Crosspool down to Racker Way (mentioned in a deed of Edward I) then to Broad Lane, Bridgehouses and over to Templeborough. The other, a pack-horse road, went from Walkley Lane to Camm Well at Camm Fields (this Well of pure spring water was supposed never to have dried up) and then over Steel Bank, where later the Heavygate Inn was built in 1689. Walkley Lane was the pack-horse route to Owlerton, to the Lepping Stones (now Leppings Lane), and to Wadsley Hall, where the Lord of the Manor of Wadsley and Owlerton lived.

Three Charters, dated 1300, 1400 and 1500 mention people in Walkley. In the list of Membra Castia De Sheffield of 1366, in the time of Edward III, the name Walkley is found. In the Charter of Queen Mary (1554), which created a Corporation named The Twelve Capital Burgesses and Commonalty of the Town and Parish of Sheffield (now called the Church Burgesses), there were several cottages and closes, or small-holdings, worked by tenants of the Lord of the Manor of Sheffield.

Later, the road that went over Steel Bank became a turnpike road and a heavy gate was placed at the point where the Heavygate Inn was later built in 1698. The first licensee of the Heavygate Inn was John Webster. He was keeper of the Tollgate. His family had farmed Steel Bank Farm years before. In the time before the Heavygate Inn was built, a survey was made by Harrison in 1637. A view from Steel Bank was mentioned where one could look down onto the town of Sheffield and see the fair Castle standing at the junction of the Don and Sheaf, the Corn Mill and the Parish Church of St. Peter.

At the time of Harrison's survey in 1637, the side roads had not been built in Walkley and South Road (as it is today) was a very narrow path called The Cutting, leading to The Spring in the Vale. In 1601 Walkley Old Hall was built by the Rawson family at the corner of Heavygate Road and Camm Street. In 1926 this was demolished when the Walkley Estate was built.

During the latter part of Mary Queen of Scots' imprisonment in Sheffield Castle, Thomas Creswick, Lord of the Manor of Owlerton and tenant of the Earl of Shrewsbury for the biggest part of Lower Walkley, also had tenancy of part of Sheffield Park. This was glorious, full of oak trees, walnut trees, herds of wild deer and extending for eight miles from the Manor so it would be quite possible that he would sometimes get a glimpse of the captive Queen in the grounds of the Manor, or even be taking part in the hunting of stags that she would watch from the flat roof of the Manor Castle.

Sheffield Castle, first built by William de Lovetot and later, after the Wars of the Barons, was rebuilt of stone by Thomas de Furnival. It was to last about 450 years. The parish church was first built by William de Lovetot, but was extended and repaired by the Talbots, the Second, Fourth and Sixth Earls of Shrewsbury.

Walkley Old Hall (built 1601 by W.M. Rawson, demolished 1926) was situated at the corner of Heavygate Road and Camm Street

A later photograph of Walkley Old Hall

Horse drawn carts at the junction of Walkley Lane and Walkley Road, 1910.

Junction of Walkley Lane and Walkley Road today. The houses in the background in 1910 have been removed and replaced with more modern residences.

Car No. 127 at Walkley tram terminus, South Road, at the junction with Palm Street in 1904.

The former terminus is now a busy road junction. The last tram ran from from Walkley Tram Terminus to the City Centre in 1956. Later the tracks were not removed, but covered over.

The Rivelin Valley

In Harrison's survey of 1637, a certain William Greaves had a wheel at Rivelin, Robert Shaw and Thomas Revell had part shares in wheels at Rivelin, where the making of scythes and cutlery was carried out and John Hoole had three acres of land and orchards just below Camm Fields. This is how we arrived at the street names.

During Elizabeth's reign and Mary Queen of Scots' fourteen year imprisonment in Sheffield, the population of Walkley and district was about 200 people, being either very poor grinders or cutlers who worked at the Wheels at Rivelin. The houses or cottages were of stone with thatched roofs. Chimneys from the centre of the floor would carry out the smoke, fuel being mainly wood and peat.

Although the work at the Mills and Wheels at Rivelin was very hard, with long working hours, probably daylight to dusk, the surroundings of Rivelin Valley were of unsurpassed beauty with massive trees, the river full of salmon, trout and eels and the woods full of game. Where Rivelin met the Loxley at Malin Bridge there was a corn mill worked by a Mr. Parkin in 1794. The water wheel stands to this day.

Just above Rivelin is a place called Little Matlock, this means 'The end of Loxley Valley'. Here, it is said, Robin Hood was born and lived before travelling on as an outlaw to Sherwood Forest. In those days he was called Robin of Loxley.

In the late 1600's there was a Farmer Cundy who lived at the Twenty Acres Farm in the area where the street now bears his name. He was a great friend of John Webster, the Heavygate Inn landlord.

The Early 1700's

In the early 1700's there were few cottages, but the ones of note which stood until recently were: (1750) the old cottages in Commonside that were knocked down in the late 1940's, old people's bungalows taking their place, and Barber Cottage in Barber Nook, built in the 1720's. In the 1930's, Mr. Kenneth Ramsall lived at Barber Cottage and had the place put in good repair. He was a teacher of music and had been round the world as the pianist in Geraldo's band. The newer cottages in Commonside have been there since the 1880's.

Barber Road was named after the Mr. Barber who built Barber Cottage. Next to it there used to be an old workhouse and House of Correction. When the tram tracks were put down in Barber Road people scoffed and said that trams would never get up there. Previously the horse buses always had to have extra horses to help pull them up.

The area around Birkendale at the top of Howard Road was first of all a private estate built in the early 1800's and planned by an Austrian who came to stay in the district. The name is derived from the German "Birkenthal", meaning 'a valley of birch trees'. There used to be many fine houses there with large families and lots of maids and coachmen.

The old turnpike roads had usually followed a route made by sheep, who always took the easiest way to get from one place to another. The roads would be covered with a layer of 'Gripton Limestones' or chippings from mill wheels.

The people who lived in Walkley before the roads were built very rarely went into the town as there were not many shops. A Journeyman or Chapman came round to the farms selling his wares and he would have 20 or 30 mules or horses. He and his friends would have protection from footpads.

Mushroom Lane was named after a man who built a house there of grass sods and stones on the waste ground at Crookesmoor. Starting after sundown and working very hard and quickly, he had his rough house built before sunrise the following morning. By the time people arrived, smoke was pouring from the chimney. The house became Mushroom Hall and the road, when it was later built, was named Mushroom Lane. The man's name was Pinder.

In those days punishment was very hard and a person could be hanged for stealing a sheep or stealing from pack horse trains and coaches. The erection of turnpike gates helped to catch culprits.

The Late 1700's

In 1777 a Land Society was formed at Steel Bank called The Second Municipal Land Society. At that time a certain William Burton, Surgeon, Apothecary and Gentleman, held all the Deeds and Titles of Land from the Earl of Surrey, Francis Howard. These had been drawn up by the Earl's estate agent, Vincent Eyre, who became very famous and had a Sheffield street named after him.

The Steel Bank lands extended beyond Springvale to a Common called Crookesmoor, where from 1711 to 1780 there was a racecourse. People would come from far and wide to watch the races from the stands. They are long gone and Standhouse Road is now in their place. When the stands were taken down the first Crookesmoor Dams were built and up to the Second World War there were four of these reservoirs. The Steel Bank Lands stretched down to South Road, then the very narrow "Cutting".

The fields had some peculiar names which were: Little Croft, Great Croft, Great Horner Flat, The Stubbing, The Great Wood (where Fir Street now is) and the Little Wood, down to Springvale, Harrison's Field, Long Field, Little Flat and Burton's Field, Organ's Stubbing, Honey Poke and the Nook Fields. Henry Whitelock and Richard Aldam were tenants as smallholders.

From William Burton the property passed to his sister, Catherine Burton of Bramley Hall, Handsworth, then to her cousins, Ino Burton and Michael Burton, Gentlemen of Royd's Mill, and also to John Fuljambe of the Manor and Lordship of Wadsley and Wadsley Hall. So all these families were related and had tenancies and all the royalties, liberties and privileges in the said town of Sheffield in the county of York.

In 1790 Michael Burton and his wife paid £2142 for the purchase of all the lands and closes adjoining the Common called Crookesmoor and right over past the Heavygate Inn to the border of Walkley Lane, which included the Great Wood, Little Wood, Great Horner Flat, the Stubbing and Well Close (at the top of Camm Fields). This land - well over 60 acres and with small holdings and stables - was purchased from the Earl of Surrey through his agent, Vincent Eyre.

The Growth of Housing in the 1800's

In 1806 Michael Burton died, as did his wife not long after. The property passed on to his nephews, Robert Bill and Ino Bill, when the negotiations were first planned for streets to be laid down. These did not come about, however, until much later in the 1850's when the property passed into the hands of Henry Barlow of the Heavygate Inn and Farms. During the time he was tenant it was stipulated that he should keep all the walls and fences in good order. He should also prevent the erection of buildings for use as slaughter houses, Tallow Maker, Chandler, Soapmaker, Boiler, Fellmonger, Dyer or Distiller. It seems that Henry Barlow was quite a rogue and amassed his money by doing anything that he could lay his hands on. In 1855 three people, George Adsett, Edward Cooper and Ino Galby borrowed the sum of £2379 from Henry Barlow to start the Fir View Land Society and the Steel Bank Society.

During the next five years all the streets in Walkley appeared practically as you see them today except Matlock Road, then called Wharncliffe Road, Fulton Road, called Prospect Street and Heavygate Road, still Steel Bank. Burgoyne Road was named after Major General Montague Burgoyne who made his name in the Crimean War. As we get to 1870, houses were being built in these streets and several old cottages were knocked down. Some of the houses in Cromwell Street, Fir Street and Greenhow Street still retained in their gardens the fruit and other trees that were part of the orchards and woods mentioned in the 18th century.

The Church

Just after the Battle of Waterloo and around the time when Wellington was Prime Minister, several large churches were built in Sheffield. These were St. Mary's Bramall Lane, St. George's and St. Phillip's. After the passing of Sir Robert Peel's Acts several more churches began to spring up and so, as Walkley became more populated, the need for a church was great.

In 1861 a Chapel of Ease or Mission Church was built at the junction of Hadfield Street and Howard Road. This was on the site of an old carpenter's shop. The Mission was led by the Rev. John Livesey, Vicar of St. Phillip's. He was also the instigator of building the Mission which cost around £1000, some of which he contributed himself, with the rest coming from an Appeal. The first Sheffield Church Extension Society then started constructing a substantial building in 1867. By 1869, St. Mary's Walkley was finished, with a 90ft spire and in the Early English decorated style, at a cost of £3200. The Archbishop of York consecrated the Church and the first Vicar was Thomas Smith. Present at the ceremony were several famous Sheffield names: Revs. J.E. Blakeney, J. Aldous, Dr. Gatty, the famous Sheffield historian and John Livesey. The clock and tower were given as a thanks offering by William Ward of Burgoyne Road. The six bells were given by Mr. W. Littlewood, coal merchant of Edward Street, who also left a legacy of £500 for ringers to ring on the anniversary of consecration. The East Window represented the Birth, Crucifixion, Resurrection and Ascension of our Lord and was given by William Turner, a steel manufacturer. A stained glass window was also given by Mr. Littlewood in memory of Roland Millington aged eight years.

St. Mary's School

Up to the time of Walkley Church being built there were no schools in Walkley other than one or two Dame Schools which gave a private education. So in 1870 when the Education Act was passed, and the Sheffield School Board was formed under the management of such prominent people as Sir John Brown and Mark Firth, St. Mary's Day School was built at a cost of £2180. The money was obtained by subscriptions and a government grant and thus was opened in 1871 in a building attached to St. Mary's Church.

When the school first opened on the 4th of December, the Master was Mr. Lewis and there were fifty-five scholars on the first day. These numbers grew rapidly so by the end of 1871 the school was full. A month after the opening the Infants' School began with Miss E. Ducker as Mistress.

These were the days of school money and fees were fixed by the School Managers. The fees ranged from one penny, 2d, 3d and 4d according to the age of the scholars and the wealth of the family. Purchasing books, pencils, pens, paper and rulers were also the responsibility of the pupils. As a result, the school tended to take in the children of better-off parents like the local shopkeepers and bigwigs of Carr Road, whilst Burgoyne Road School would take in the children of less well off families.

It was not until 1883 that an assistant teacher was engaged. Later, pupil teachers were introduced, but monitors, who were paid a shilling a week, also helped. Each year one of Her Majesty's School Inspectors came and carried out thorough examinations. Financial grants to the school depended on the Inspector's examination. The Head Teacher's work was not confined to the school, the Pupil Teachers had to attend his house at night for further instruction and sometimes in the morning before school.

The school remained attached to St. Mary's Church until July 1978, when it moved to it's current location in between Cundy Street and Burgoyne Road, which became available when Burgoyne Road School moved to new premises to become Walkley Primary School. In 1991 the school was almost closed after a proposal by Sheffield Eductaion Authority. However, the school survived and has continued to grow since.

Conditions in School

For several years the boys, and later even the girls, were taught drill by Sergeant Green of Her Majesty's 35th Regiment of Foot, who was stationed at Hillsborough Barracks. (In 1890 there were two Regiments at Hillsborough Barracks, one of Infantry and one of Cavalry and there was accommodation for 918 men, 56 Officers and also stabling for a hundred horses).

Later on, Sergeant Green was replaced by Sergeant Major Lockey. These were hard days for the children and quite a lot of truancy appeared in the registers on drill days. Also, when Barnum and Bailey's Circus came there was an absence of scholars. Several times little parties made up their minds to have time off and go to see the bears in the pit at the Botanical Gardens.

When Mr. Chester began his teaching, conditions were a little lax, but he soon changed this. He was a great disciplinarian and very strict and it was not long before the school was working in top gear. Quite a lot of the Senior Citizens of Walkley will remember Mr. Chester and a lot of the things that they were taught.

By 1890 all school fees were abolished and everything was supplied by the Education Committee. Some of the teachers well remembered are Mr. Shaw, Mr. Prideaux, Miss E. Brown and Miss Button.

Around the 1880's more schools were built in the area, including Bolehill School, Greaves Street and Morley Street. In 1893 the average attendance at St. Mary's was 283 scholars, meaning that classes of forty children were quite common.

Other Public Buildings

In the 1905 property was knocked down at the end of South Road and the Library was built. The library was paid for by Andrew Carnegie, whose benefactions exceeded £70million, including public libraries throughout the USA and Britain.

The first hospital in the area was the Sheffield Infirmary which was built in the 1790's. One of the most famous people to be on the Committee was Florence Nightingale whose family lived at Broomhill. Other people on the Committee of the Infirmary were Mark-Firth, Sir John Brown and The Duke of Norfolk. The two most famous physicians were Dr. Cocking and Dr. W. Porter.

In the early days leeches which were used for blood-letting were supplied and bred by a chemist called Mr. Cocking of Barkers Pool. It is said that in one year he supplied over a thousand leeches to the Royal Infirmary.

Banks

In the Banking business, several private banks were owned in Sheffield from 1780 onwards, such as William Shore's and Henry Broadbent's. The first Yorkshire Penny Bank opened in Church Street in 1878 and later a branch opened at Walkley in the early 1900's.

Tramcar No. 44 on Walkley route at the junction of South Road and Fulton Road in 1899.

None of the buildings in the original picture now remain, replaced by modern housing and green space.

South Road and the corner of Freedom Road 1906.

The wall of the building at the top of Freedom Road has
been rebuilt fairly recently, but otherwise the buildings
have remained much the same.

Laying of tram tracks on Howard Road, Walkley 1890.

The tramlines having been layed and removed again, the landscape is almost identical over 100 years later.

St. Mary's Church, corner of Hadfield Street. Looking towards South Road 1915.

The church has remained near identical for over 100 years, whilst South Road has changed around it a great deal.

Walkley Library, laying of the foundation stone, building
works by D. O'Neill & Sons Ltd. 1904

Walkley Library, corner of Walkley Road and South Road
1908

With the exception of the removal of the small tower above the doors, the library has not changed since being built. The library remains the central hub of Walkley life.

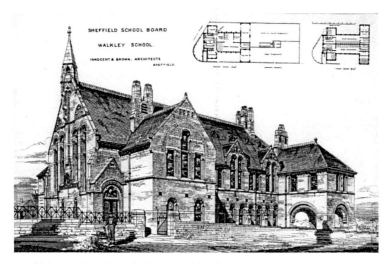

Walkley School, original architects design.

And the School as it looks today. Notice the open arches in the initial design to the right of the building have now been closed off to create an additional room.

South Road, Walkley looking towards Tram 160 and St. Mary's Church.

The building is now the Walkley Centre, part of Sheffield College.

John Shore, who started the banking business in Campo Lane, was the grandfather of Florence Nightingale and Shore House at Fulwood is named after him. Henry Broadbent had a bank in Campo Lane and his son, Thomas Broadbent, built a house at the bottom of York Street which remains to this day. He also built and developed one side of Paradise Square.

Later the Sheffield Savings Bank opened in Walkley and in the years between the two wars, Walkley was a very busy shopping centre.

John Ruskin (1821 - 1910)

 Though not a Sheffielder by birth, the famous author, poet, art collector and philanthropist John Ruskin will forever live on in the city through the Ruskin Art Gallery. In the middle of the 1800's he settled in Sheffield and later had a house built in Walkley on Bolehill Road called Ruskin House. He said that his house looking over the Rivelin Valley had one of the most beautiful views in the country, next to his favourite view in the Lake District.

Ruskin founded the Guild of St George in 1871 which in turn founded the St George's Museum at his house in Walkley. The museum was created so that the 'working man' would be able to enjoy and benefit from seeing this wide-ranging collection which included prints, plaster casts, drawings, illuminated manuscripts, books, minerals, geological specimens and coins. When Ruskin set up the museum, he called it the "Museum of St George", and it was one of four sites of the Guild of St George, a body which existed to promulgate the views of Ruskin. By 1890 the museum had outgrown the Walkley cottage and was moved to Meersbrook Park.

The Ruskin House at Walkley was taken over in the 1880's by a committee of gentlemen as a home for girls. The gentlemen on the Board were prominent people such as Sir Henry Stevenson, John Wycliffe-Wilson and W. Osborne-Priestman. Girls in the home would be between the ages of twelve and sixteen, mostly orphans or destitute. There were 46 girls, looked after by two house-mothers and a matron. This home continued on up to the Second World War, when it was used as a communications centre for Civil Defence. Later it was turned into flats.

Public Transport

There was no transport in Walkley much before the 1870's, at least not for the ordinary working man. The gentry used horse-back, light gigs or traps (a kind of very light coach).

In 1873 the first horse buses arrived and they were privately owned. Reuben Thompson of Glossop Road started a service from Glossop Road to Springvale and it was rather difficult up the incline of Barber Road. A cab with three horses abreast was used, and in winter time a lead horse was always waiting at the bottom by Harcourt Road to give them that extra pull. The road across the tip as we know it, from Mushroom Lane to Harcourt Road, had only just been built. Before this it was a valley level with the boating dam. The drivers and conductors worked very long hours. In 1880 a hundred hours a week earned one the princely sum of 25 shillings (£1.25) and the conductor received 12 shillings (60p) per week.

The first trams to Walkley were in the 1890's and were single deckers and still only went as far as Springvale, but were later extended to South Road. The trams improved in design as the years went on and by the 1960's, when it was time for them to be replaced by buses, they were really elegant. The trams did great service during both wars, and in the Second World War rarely stopped, except for the blitzes, when so many of them were destroyed or badly damaged.

The Walkley Palladium

The Walkley Palladium theatre opened on 17 December 1914 with a seating capacity of 1000 with an impressive balcony which extended along three sides of the auditorium. The first films showed on the opening night included Brewster's Millions, news stories, a sketch caricaturing the German Kaiser and a cartoon. Performances were at 6.50pm and 9.00pm with Saturday matinees at 2.30pm.

Talking movies were introduced on 25 November 1929; Walkley Palladium was the sixth cinema in Sheffield to be wired for sound and the fourth to install the Western Electric system. The first talking film was The Rainbow Man, which was very popular at the time.

Various improvements were made over the years including the hand painting of Lakeland scenes, with lanterns suspended from the golden ceiling moulding. Sunday opening was introduced in May 1953 to be replaced by Bingo in May 1962. The cinema closed on 6 October 1962 after 48 years with a double bill of Gaolbreak with John Mills and Tiara Tahiti with James Mason.

The Postal Service

The first pillar boxes were installed in 1855 and the postal round for postmen was very gruelling indeed, especially in the Walkley, Crookes and Ranmoor areas. One famous postman, John Westerman, was born in 1824 and died in 1904 and worked 40 years as a carrier. He was classified in the Sheffield Directory of 1871 and his round covered 22 miles from Ranmoor over the Mayfield Valley and Crimicar Lane. The uniforms were quite different from today, with a little 'pork pie' hat and leather belt with pouches for telegrams.

Life in Walkley before World War I

From 1900 up to the First World War there were great events taking place. There was no such thing as television and the wireless was in its infancy, with sets fed by an accumulator. In the back gardens there used to be forests of poles carrying aerials.

One of the main events was the Resurrection Service at the Walkley Cemetery. Another was the Empire Day Celebration on May 24th (in those days the Empire spanned a fifth of the whole world), and also the great football and cricket matches played by the schools; Burgoyne Road won many cups and shields.

The Resurrection Service was on Easter Sunday and first instigated by Reverend T. Smith. For many years on that day the trams would be crammed with people. It was reported in the Sheffield Independent that in 1910 over 10,000 people attended the Resurrection Service, headed by a full brass band, choir wearing mortar boards, church-wardens and other dignitaries with top hats. There was always a barrow covered with a white sheet for people to throw their collection into.

A popular event was Whit-Monday Sunday School gatherings. Most schools other than St. Mary's went to the Parks to sing and of course there was always a great gathering and the day always seemed to turn out to be hot. St. Mary's congregation would parade round the parish led by the Scout band, calling at the houses of parishioners who were ill or disabled. Afterwards there was a gathering at the Vicarage where they had lemonade and biscuits. At this time, one must not forget probably the greatest Sheffield musician of all time, Sir. H. Coward. His choirs were world famous. The Sheffield Choir of 1924 broke all records for choral singing and this great man certainly kept up the tradition that James Montgomery started when he founded the Sunday School movement and had the Montgomery Hall built.

Walkley Home Life in the 1930's

The lighting in Walkley houses was by oil lamps at the beginning of the 20th century but later the changeover was made to gas. In a house at night you would find the light given by a gas bracket on the wall or by twin arms suspended from the ceiling. When the mantles were lit they emitted a little swishing sound. The street lighting was by gas lamp as well, and it was a common sight to see the old lamplighter going round with his ladder lighting the street lamps. Those scholars who were taught by Fred Chester at St. Mary's will remember the poem he taught them, "The Lamplighter".

Most homes only had one tap on the stone sink. This was cold water and if one wanted any hot there was a little water boiler at the side of the Yorkshire range which was heated by coal. The range was black-leaded and always kept shining. On wash-day the housewife would be up at 5am to light a fire with wood under the copper or set-pot in the corner of the kitchen, then the clothes would be put in a dolly tub and a "peggy-leg" used to swish the clothes backwards and forwards (many remember from their childhood how hard and tiring this could be). The ironing would be done with a flat-iron heated in front of the fire and if it was too hot, soap would be rubbed on it so that the clothes would not burn.

Most children wore boots (shoes had not come into fashion). Boys would generally have studs in their boots and steel tips to make them last longer. They had great fun sliding and seeing what sparks they could make.

Sanitation was very primitive at first, there was no such thing as an indoor toilet. Toilets were outside and consisted of a wooden seat covering a bin which would have to be emptied periodically by men who came at night to do the work. They were called Night Soil Men. Some of the toilets even had places for two or three people, especially in the country districts. It was a real boon to families when flush toilets came into being, although up to the Second World War not many houses had indoor toilets.

Bathing used to be a primitive affair: mainly a zinc bath would be used and, hot water being scarce, one lot would be used by all the family. Although wages were very low, mainly about 30 shillings a week, food was very cheap with a loaf at 3d, corned beef 2d per quarter, cheese 6d per pound, meat about a shilling a pound and milk 2d a pint, all this in old shillings and pennies.

The First World War, which lasted four years, brought great sadness to Walkley because after the battles of the Somme on July 1st, 1916, many families were bereaved. On the War Memorial in St. Mary's are the names of 251 men who died in the terrible carnage of Flanders Fields.

Between 1930 and 1938 there was a great depression and lots of men were out of work. These were the breadwinners and in those days not many women went out to work, they looked after the house. Children leaving school at 13 or 14 years used to be errand boys for tiny wages. There was no such thing as teenagers (as we know them today), children grew up and as soon as they reached 21 were then men or ladies. Most children after school would go to night school and college after the day's work. Most houses had a piano and the families that were without a wireless used to make do with singing round the piano.

The time when Sheffield Wednesday won the FA Cup in 1935 was exciting, with the town absolutely packed and the team travelling on an open-top bus. This was the year of King George V and Queen Mary's Silver Jubilee, with the streets decorated with flags and a decorated tramcar running on all the routes. The weather was perfect, a heatwave to be exact.

Each time an event was held such as Sheffield Week, and later Dig for Victory and Wings for Victory, there were always decorated tramcars and Walkley terminus was always a venue for one of these. Sometimes tram drivers who were not very careful used to over-drive at the end of the terminus. The tram would go down the slope and have to be towed back. One witness claims to have seen this happen twice.

In the days of the late 1930's there were lots of activities in Walkley with good Scout groups. At one time Rev. Guy Cook was Rover Leader and Canon Rawlings Scoutmaster. Some will remember him and Spanner Hayes, Alan Hewitt, Frank Sheldon, Harry Harrap and Philip Fletcher. There was a large Guide Company, led by Miss Selby and Ethel Drury. There was a flourishing Girls' Friendly Society, led by Miss Hilda Cutts and, of course, we had the TOC H Society, led by Rev. Sorby-Briggs as Padre. This was for the men and any veterans of the First World War. Meetings were held in the old barn at the back of Mrs. Middleham's, The Hollies, a large house at the bottom of Springvale Road and corner of Heavygate. Later this was demolished by a direct hit from a land mine in 1940.

The Second World War

So we come to the six years of the Second World War. This cannot be passed without saying something about it. Of course, it will be news for the younger people, but memories for the older people. The Civil Defence was called together in the Munich scare of 1938. By the time war was actually declared, the Civil Defence had been trained at Ranmoor College, in fire-fighting, first-aid , going through the gas van to distinguish different poison gases, night exercises and training to drive Civil Defence Ambulances, so that on that day of 3rd September 1939 they were ready for almost any eventuality.

"The first day of the war was a beautiful September day. We had been to St. Mary's Morning Service, it was a Sunday, and coming along South Road one could see all the barrage balloons flying high, something that gave you a little shiver, in the pit of the stomach, making you wonder what was going to happen".
Albert Staley

The first six months were a 'phoney war' with not a lot of action, except of course that men were being called up and there was the blackout. In blackout trams ran along South Road at night with very dim lighting and netting stuck on the windows with drivers struggling to see with no road lights allowed. People had to carry gas masks and service personnel had to carry steel helmets, these included police, fire brigade, etc.

There were several large air raid shelters (other than the Anderson shelters in most people's back gardens). One of these was under the Howard Road Conservative Club and one at Dr. Lahiff's (now the Walkley Medical Centre). This one contained beds and other facilities for the bombed-out and was used quite a lot after the blitzes. In the early days of the war a lot of the children from the schools in Walkley were evacuated to places in Derbyshire and Cheshire. Trams were crowded with children with their gas-masks and little cases of belongings going to the railway station. When one looked across to Stannington from the Bolehills there was hardly any built-up area and Wood Lane was all fields. A heavy anti-aircraft gun site was put there to defend the Western area. Church services at all places of worship were usually just in the mornings and at all times one had to be ready to leave in case of air raids. There were no football matches at Owlerton and Bramall Lane until the latter end of the war, and the Sheffield United ground became very badly bomb-damaged.

Enemy action first started in Sheffield in June 1940 and the first bombs were dropped in Mushroom Lane and Dovercourt Road. From then on until the winter, the raids were spasmodic and then the nightly raids began with the bombing of London, Coventry, Hull and Manchester. Then on December 12th it was Sheffield's turn and the alert was received at 6.30pm. By 7pm the first wave of bombers dropped thousands of incendiary bombs up and down the main thoroughfares; The Moor, The Haymarket, Castle Street, The Wicker and Neepsend. By the time the heavy bombers came in the next wave there were many fires, and then until 4am it was wave after wave every half-hour. In all about 300 bombers took part on the Thursday night and 200 on the Sunday night.

South Road, Walkley, March 1956

Whilst the road and vehicles have changed quite a lot, the buildings have altered little over the 47-year period.

Up to the 1920's the Walkley Palladium Picture House would show silent films, but after 1928 these became 'talkies'. It was 6d downstairs and 9d in the balcony and one could book seats as well. The photo above was taken in 1914.

The theatre was lost shortly after the war and is now a modern supermarket.

Incidents in Walkley came about 10.30pm to 12pm when land mines were dropped in Heavygate Road, Springvale Road, Bloor Street, Whitehouse Lane, Rivelin, Mushroom Lane and all along the Infirmary Road area. The Jessop Hospital, Weston Park Museum, Neepsend Gas Works and St. Michael's Neepsend were all hit and the Wood Lane anti aircraft guns did a lot of roof damage with shrapnel but only credited two planes shot down. Part of one fell at the top of Greenhow Street, but was quickly cleared away. A land mine was dropped by parachute above Walkley Church and exploded prematurely about 500ft up, doing quite a bit of roof damage. It was lucky it didn't explode on the ground or there would have been no St. Mary's Church or school! The green silk parachute was retrieved and kept in the Warden's Post until the end of the war. After the blitz there were a few more minor raids but these gradually ceased. When the end of the war came in May 1945, V.E.Day, Walkley was one mass of flags and there were bonfires and street parties.

Post-War Walkley

In the February of 1961 there was a hurricane which did a lot of damage to the Church and the Church Hall. There was quite a lot of controversy at the time about having a new Church Hall, but this died out through lack of funds. During the time of Rev. Hubert George and Rev. Stanley Archer Clark, the Church had a house in Palm Street and one in Parsonage Street and for a time had a parish worker who lived in Parsonage Street.

During the 1950's and 1960's there was a great move in the population of Walkley, lots of families went to live at Crosspool and Lodge Moor when the area there was being built up and so the face of Walkley was gradually changing.

After the war Walkley lost such places as the Walkley Palladium, Dr. Lahiff's house was made into a Medical Centre and his front garden had shops built on. The Howard Road Chapel was used as a warehouse and shops such as Hawksfords, the Maypole, Davy's, Wibberley's and the famous chemist Boot's all disappeared. The old Boot's is now Vito's Italian restaurant.

Today the shopping area of Walkley has significantly decreased caused by the appearance of Supermarkets and cheap transport. Many shops have now been turned into houses although a selection of successful businesses still trade daily.

In the lower part of Walkley, major changes have been made. Quite a lot of old property in the region of Harworth Street, Harold Street and towards Whitehouse Lane has disappeared. New flats and old people's bungalows have been built. The main part of Walkley, such as South Road and Howard Road, still retains its character as a village separate from the town part of Sheffield, as it did a hundred and fifty years ago.